WORLD BANK WORKING PAPER NO. 132

Environmental Policies and Strategic Communication in Iran

The Value of Public Opinion Research in Decisionmaking

Daniele Calabrese
Khalil Kalantari
Fabio M. Santucci
Elena Stanghellini

THE WORLD BANK
Washington, D.C.

World Bank Working Papers are published to communicate the results of the Bank's work to the development community with the least possible delay. The manuscript of this paper therefore has not been prepared in accordance with the procedures appropriate to formally-edited texts. Some sources cited in this paper may be informal documents that are not readily available.

The findings, interpretations, and conclusions expressed herein are those of the author(s) and do not necessarily reflect the views of the International Bank for Reconstruction and Development/The World Bank and its affiliated organizations, or those of the Executive Directors of The World Bank or the governments they represent.

The World Bank does not guarantee the accuracy of the data included in this work. The boundaries, colors, denominations, and other information shown on any map in this work do not imply any judgment on the part of The World Bank of the legal status of any territory or the endorsement or acceptance of such boundaries.

The material in this publication is copyrighted. Copying and/or transmitting portions or all of this work without permission may be a violation of applicable law. The International Bank for Reconstruction and Development/The World Bank encourages dissemination of its work and will normally grant permission promptly to reproduce portions of the work.

For permission to photocopy or reprint any part of this work, please send a request with complete information to the Copyright Clearance Center, Inc., 222 Rosewood Drive, Danvers, MA 01923, USA, Tel: 978-750-8400, Fax: 978-750-4470, www.copyright.com.

All other queries on rights and licenses, including subsidiary rights, should be addressed to the Office of the Publisher, The World Bank, 1818 H Street NW, Washington, DC 20433, USA, Fax: 202-522-2422, email: pubrights@worldbank.org.

ISBN-13: 978-0-8213-7421-4
eISBN: 978-0-8213-7422-1
ISSN: 1726-5878   DOI: 10.1596/978-0-8213-7421-4

Daniele Calabrese is a Communications Officer in the Development Communications Unit of the External Affairs Department of the World Bank. Khalil Kalantari is at the University of Tehran. Fabio M. Santucci and Elena Stanghellini are at the University of Perugia.

Library of Congress Cataloging-in-Publication Data

Environmental policies and strategic communication in Iran : the value of public opinion research in decision making / Daniele Calabrese . . . [et al.].
    p. cm.
  ISBN 978-0-8213-7421-4
  1. Environmental policy--Iran. 2. Public opinion polls--Iran. 3. Decision making--Iran.
I. Calabrese, Daniele.
  GE190.I7E58 2008
  363.700955--dc22

                                                              2007049141

Contents

Introduction

In recent years due to its geography, industries and traffic, air pollution in Tehran has become a major problem. Most private and public vehicles are old and have no emission control systems. The Municipality of Tehran and the Department of Environment have acted in several ways to reduce pollution, and communication activities are part of their strategy. For better planning and for possible monitoring and evaluation of the communication activities, a baseline study took place in 2004 with direct interviews of 1,200 Tehran residents. The interviews covered the residents' experiences, opinions, knowledge and willingness to act. Use of and trust in several information sources and media were also investigated to select the best communication mix for future communication activities.

Background

Greater Tehran extends over an area of about 700 km² and currently has 12 million inhabitants. The annual rainfall is about 230 mm, concentrated in six months. The annual mean temperature is 17°C, ranging from 39°C in summer to −6°C in winter. About 1.5 million tons of air pollutants are produced in Tehran annually, mostly consisting of carbon monoxide from the nearly two million circulating cars—a large percentage of which are very old, with poor fuel efficiency and without catalytic converters. Air pollution is made worse by Tehran's geographic position: the mountains in the north trap the pollutants, which hover over the town in windless periods. Tehran's high altitude, between 1,100 and 1,800 meters, makes fuel combustion inefficient.

Additionally over the past decades of urbanization and industrialization, the city's green areas have largely been destroyed. For all of these reasons, Tehran has become one of the most polluted cities in the world with all of the associated consequences on the health of its inhabitants. Several efforts have been made by the National Government, the Department of Environment (DOE) and the Municipality of Tehran (MOT) to reduce the air pollution: new legislation and standards, strengthened controls, environmental studies, elaboration of an environmental master plan and its partial implementation.

CHAPTER 1

Objectives of the Study

The Government of Iran is currently implementing a five-year project, co-financed by the World Bank, which aims: a) to strengthen the institutional capacity to monitor air and water quality, b) to build partnerships among ministries, universities, municipalities and civil societies, and c) to strengthen training and public awareness on environmental issues. In order to design a proper communication campaign, a study was planned to establish a baseline (in terms of knowledge, attitudes and behaviors) to assess the efficacy of future actions and to explore which communication sources and channels are the most effective for reaching the different population groups. The need for such a communication strategy relies upon the assumption—proven in studies in western countries—that public environmental knowledge is generally low (Arcury and Johnson 1987).

Numerous studies over two decades have examined the associations between environmentalism and standard social structural categories. These studies reveal some factors such as age and education that are consistently related to environmentalism over time and across studies. In fact, the strongest and most consistent predictor of environmentalism is age. The effects of age are conceptually distinct and cannot be disentangled in a single cross-sectional study (Buttel and Taylor 1979). Education, political ideology and place of residence also are consistently related to environmental concern. Links to other social structural variables, such as income, class, and occupation or industrial sector, are weak, seldom statistically significant, and show no consistent pattern across studies. The relationship between gender and environmental concern has been more carefully theorized than other demographic variables. Women are generally more concerned than men, and the literature explores several possible mediating factors. One is gendered difference in the experience and effects of parenthood. For men, parenthood leads to less environmental concern, for women to greater concern (Stern and others 1993).

Some studies also suggest a weak yet positive relationship with some measures of religious participation. Other literature links indicators of environmentalism to social psychological factors, identifying a wide range of correlates including attitudes, beliefs, values, and world views. This generally supports the conclusion that broad values and attitudes are predictive of specific ones and indicates that the most important social psychological factors depend on the type of behavior (for instance, the predictors of support for political action may be different from those of pro-environmental consumer behavior). Support for the broad goals of the environmental movement is consistently associated with expectation of harmful consequences to the environment and acceptance of the "New Ecological Paradigm" (Dunlap and others 1978).

By comparison with this literature, little research links the social psychological correlates of environmentalism to social structure. Such research might show how environmental attitudes are shaped by social context and reveal some of the mechanisms by which social structural variables influence environmentally relevant behavior. One example of such research is the literature that explores how particular religious beliefs might mediate between denomination and environmentalism. These studies explore the possibility that religion may shape environmentalism through indirect effects on beliefs, attitudes, and values. They illustrate a conceptual strategy of explaining environmentalism as a joint product of social structure, socialization, and social psychological processes. Several studies show that a cognitive hierarchy framework consisting of basic values, general beliefs, specific attitudes, and behavior provides a suitable basis for understanding environmentalism. General beliefs in turn influence specific attitudes, and these in turn influence specific actions or behaviors (Schultz and Zelezny 1999).

Although the effect of knowledge is not conclusive, there have been several studies suggesting that knowledge plays an important role in enhancing the environmental attitude and behavior relationship by providing individuals with the ability to better formulate alternate views and present arguments to support their beliefs and behaviors. Antecedent factors such as social structural variables and socialization influences have been associated with value orientation, attitudes and environmental behaviors. Of social structural variables, women, people with higher levels of education, younger individuals, urban residents and those with a liberal political orientation are more prone to support the principles of sustainable resource management (McFarlane and Boxall 2003).

Though individuals perceive the deterioration of their environmental conditions, they still need to be convinced about the positive effects of their behavior. In western countries, many studies have been performed to reveal the reasons that lead people to act responsibly towards the environment (Cottrell and Graefe 1997; Keiser, Woelfing, and Fuhrer 1999). For a study in Turkey, see Tuna (2004). This body of research can be seen as the first step in this direction.

CHAPTER 2

Research Methodology

This article reports the main findings of a survey conducted on the perception, knowledge, and behavior of Tehran residents, relating to the environment. The sampling design was stratified based on gender and area of residence. For each stratum, about 200 people were interviewed. This number is considered large enough for the estimates to be accurate, according to statistical laws of convergence (see the derivations in Hansen, Hurwitz, and Medow [1953]). The interview was supported by a structured questionnaire containing 25 questions, including six Likert-type scales. During a three-day workshop in Teheran, the questionnaire and the interview procedures were elaborated with a participatory approach (Laws, Harper, and Marcus 2003). The workshop, "Communication on Environmental Problems," was managed by the authors and attended by about 20 managers and staff members of the DOE of which about half were women. A pilot study was conducted to test the questionnaire, and two questions were modified consequently.

To intercept representative people of the resident population, interviews took place in public parks in North, Central and South Tehran on two consecutive weekends in June 2004 (Table 1). Randomly chosen, interviewers asked 1,200 individuals about their environmental behaviors, opinions, knowledge, and sources of information. The interviews were performed by 25 students of social sciences selected and trained for this purpose. In order to achieve the target number of 1,200 questionnaires, a total of 1,403 people had to be stopped for an interview. This implies a non-response rate of 14.5 percent, which can be considered acceptable. The results were transferred into a database and analyzed through SPSS 11 and through SPLUS 5.0.

This article reveals and comments on only a few of the study's most relevant findings: respondents' perceptions, preparedness to act, knowledge of institutional aspects, behavior

Table 1. Final Sample, by Area and Gender

Area	Men no.				Women no.				All no.*			
	S	R	I	NRR	S	R	I	NRR	S	R	I	NRR
North	218	18	200	8.3	223	29	194	13.0	441	47	394	10.7
Center	231	29	202	12.6	231	38	193	16.5	462	67	395	14.5
South	234	33	201	14.1	240	46	194	19.2	474	79	395	16.7
Total	683	80	603	11.7	694	113	581	16.3	1377	193	1,184	14.0

S = stopped; R = refused to answer; I = interviewed; NRR = non-response rate (R/S $\times$ 100) as percent age.
* = there were 16 questionnaires with uncomplete information.

relating to environmental problems, and information sources and channels. A second study, specifically focusing the linkages between knowledge about air quality and behavior, was also performed.

Composition of the Sample

The sample consisted of 51 percent men and 49 percent women of whom 63 percent were under 30 years of age, 35 percent were between 31 and 60, and only 2 percent were over 60. Education levels included 43 percent with a graduate degree, 23 percent with a bachelor's degree, 11 percent attended high school and 12 percent secondary school, with other levels of formal education at lower percentages. Main occupations were 21 percent students, 18 percent private employees, 16 percent public employees, 4 percent industrial workers and 5 percent specialists. Of the respondents, 21 percent (0.8 percent of men and 42 percent of women) declared house affairs as their occupation. Income responses included 44 percent claiming no personal income, 15 percent with a monthly income below one million rials, 23 percent between one and two million rials, 12 percent between two and three million rials and 6 percent over this level.

CHAPTER 3

Main Findings

Perceptions of Environmental Problems

In relative terms when compared with other issues, environmental concerns do not appear to be a priority for the great majority of the respondents. Thirty-one percent of total respondents (34 percent men and 29 percent women) think political problems are important or very important (Table 2). Economic development is next with 6 percent of people (6.4 percent men and 5.3 percent women) perceiving it as important or very important, while inflation is similarly rated by 6.4 percent of respondents (5.8 percent of men and 6.5 percent of women).

Environmental problems are reported as important or very important by only 4 percent of respondents (4.4 percent men and 3.3 percent women).

Moreover, a large share—34 percent of respondents of both genders—believe that environmental problems are not important at all, and 53 percent do not have any opinion regarding their importance. Housing and job opportunities are also identified at a lower level of importance by both genders.

When specifically asked about some environmental issues (Table 3), however, the people of Tehran exhibit concerns about the negative consequences of pollution with water pollution being the most crucial issue.

Considering the answer by gender, 62.3 percent of men and 61.3 percent of women are very worried about water quality. Air pollution follows closely with 59.8 percent of men and 60.1 percent of women responding as very worried about pollution from cars, and 41.5 percent of men and 47.1 percent of women responding similarly to industrial pollution. Relevant responses of very worried are registered regarding noise pollution (39.5 percent men and 41.8 percent women), continuous reduction of green areas (51.3 percent men and 51.3 percent women), disposal of industrial waste (43.3 percent

Table 2. Opinions about Various Social and Economic Issues

Social Issues	Very Important		Important		Not so Important		Not Important		No Opinion		Total	
	No.	%	No.	%	No.	%	No.	%	No.	%	No.	%
Job opportunities	9	0.8	33	2.8	74	6.2	290	24.2	791	66.1	1,197	100.0
Economic development	30	2.5	40	3.3	114	9.5	453	37.9	558	48.7	1,185	100.0
Inflation	30	2.5	46	3.9	94	7.9	320	26.9	698	58.8	1,155	100.0
Environmental problems	15	1.3	32	2.7	103	8.6	408	34.1	638	53.3	1,196	100.0
Housing	13	1.1	17	1.4	58	4.8	234	19.5	878	73.1	1,197	100.0
Political problems	135	11.3	240	20.1	290	24.2	263	22	268	22.4	1,196	100.0

Table 3. Worries about Environmental Problems

How much are you personally worried about		Total										
	No Opinion		Not Worried at all		Not so Worried		Worried		Very Worried		Total	
	No.	%	No.	%	No.	%	No.	%	No.	%	No.	%
1) Air pollution caused by industries	47	3.9	24	2.0	195	16.3	403	33.6	531	44.3	1,200	100.0
2) Air pollution caused by transportation	11	.9	15	1.3	137	11.4	317	26.4	720	60.0	1,200	100.0
3) Noise pollution	34	2.8	95	7.9	237	19.8	349	29.1	485	40.4	1,200	100.0
4) Reduction of green areas	13	1.1	48	4.0	178	14.8	345	28.8	616	51.3	1,200	100.0
5) Water pollution	18	1.5	36	3.0	148	12.3	258	21.5	740	61.7	1,200	100.0
6) Industrial waste	69	5.8	43	3.6	240	20.0	341	28.4	507	42.3	1,200	100.0
7) House garbage	25	2.1	57	4.8	205	17.1	370	30.8	543	45.3	1,200	100.0

men and 41.2 percent women) and household garbage (40.5 percent men and 50.2 percent women).

The respondents showed mixed environmental attitudes, as illustrated in Table 4. More than 56 percent strongly agree or agree that "many of the claims about environmental problems are exaggerated," but on the other hand, almost 84 percent fully agree or agree that "interfering with nature has bad consequences," and almost 80 percent strongly agree or agree that "most activities are harmful to natural environment." There is a general belief that technical progress and modern technologies will help solve environmental problems, but only 33.3 percent agree or strongly agree with the statement, "The environmental situation will be better in future."

According to gender 40.5 percent of men and 37.6 percent of women strongly agree, "It is possible to have good economic growth and protect the environment at the same time." Only 8.7 percent of men and 10.5 percent of women strongly agree that "the environmental situation will be better in the future," while 31.3 percent of men and 26.8 percent of women disagree with this statement. Moreover, 37.9 percent of men and 35.7 percent of women strongly agree with the statement that "interfering with nature has bad consequences" and 36.1 percent of men and 35.7 percent of women strongly agree that "industrial activities in the suburbs can lead to irretrievable damage to the urban environment." On the other hand, 60.6 percent of men and 58.1 percent of women strongly disagree or disagree that "humans have the right to modify the natural environment to suit their needs."

Respondents are quite aware that legislation plays a key role in the protection of the environment and almost 50 percent consider that the current legislation is not adequate (Table 5); 77.4 percent strongly agree or agree that legislation could be considered adequate, but that enforcement is poor. There is a generalized consensus about the need for more legislation, which could orient the decisions of both ordinary people and of companies. In both cases, more than 85 percent of respondents agree with the call for better legislation.

Taking gender into consideration, only 9 percent of men and 11.2 percent of women believe that current legislation is adequate for preventing environmental degradation. In contrast, 40.8 percent of men and 41.2 percent of women strongly agree with the statement, "Government should pass more laws to oblige companies and ordinary people to protect the environment."

Preparedness to Act

The questionnaire used six items designed to measure how much Tehran citizens are prepared to act for environmental protection (Table 6). The statement, "The government should reduce environmental problems without charging any money from the people," elicits strong agreement from 40.2 percent of men and 37.5 percent of women. On the other hand, only 18.9 percent of men and 23.5 percent of women strongly agree, "everybody should care for the environment, even if it costs money." These responses indicate that men, more than women, believe that protection of environment is a duty of the government. Overall, results of the survey show that people are ready to give time or to organize

Table 4. Environmental Attitudes

Statements	Total											
	Strongly Agree		Agree		Neither Agree nor Disagree		Disagree		Strongly Disagree		Total	
	No.	%	No.	%	No.	%	No.	%	No.	%	No.	%
1) Many of the claims about environmental Problems are exaggerated.	243	20.3	437	36.4	216	18.0	236	19.7	68	5.7	1,200	100.0
2) Interfering with nature has bad consequences	440	36.7	565	47.1	100	8.3	74	6.2	21	1.8	1,200	100.0
3) Modern technology can solve environmental problems.	212	17.7	436	36.3	237	19.8	259	21.6	56	4.7	1,200	100.0
4) Solving the present economic problems is more important than caring about the future environment.	324	27.0	312	26.0	153	12.8	313	26.1	98	8.2	1,200	100.0
5) Most activities in modern life are harmful to the natural environment.	340	28.3	595	49.6	126	10.5	111	9.3	28	2.3	1,200	100.0
6) Humans have the right to modify the natural environment to suit their needs.	133	11.1	240	20.0	116	9.7	474	39.5	237	19.8	1,200	100.0
7) Industrial activities in the suburbs can lead to irretrievable damage to the urban environment.	445	37.1	538	44.8	112	9.3	81	6.8	24	2.0	1,200	100.0
8) Urban environmental improvements must be made regardless of their cost.	327	27.3	448	37.3	135	11.3	231	19.3	59	4.9	1,200	100.0
9) The environmental situation will be better in the future.	114	9.5	286	23.8	294	24.5	350	29.2	156	13.0	1,200	100.0
10) It is possible to have good economic growth and to protect the environment at the same time.	470	39.2	570	47.5	91	7.6	50	4.2	19	1.6	1,200	100.0

Table 5. Opinions about Environmental Legislation

Statements	Strongly Agree		Agree		Neither Agree nor Disagree		Disagree		Strongly Disagree		Total	
	No.	%	No.	%	No.	%	No.	%	No.	%	No.	%
1) Current legislation about the environment is adequate for preventing environmental degradation.	122	10.5	254	21.2	225	18.8	491	40.9	108	9.0	1,200	100.0
2) There is good legislation about the environment, but it is not completely enforced.	342	28.5	587	48.9	145	12.1	106	8.8	20	1.7	1,200	100.0
3) Government should pass more laws to make ordinary people protect the environment.	489	40.8	537	44.8	99	8.3	57	4.8	18	1.5	1,200	100.0
4) Government should pass more laws making business protect the environment.	492	41.0	537	44.8	101	8.4	50	4.2	20	1.7	1,200	100.0

Table 6. Preparedness to Act

Statements	Total												
	Strongly Agree		Agree		Neither Agree nor Disagree		Disagree		Strongly Disagree		Total	
	No.	%	No.	%	No.	%	No.	%	No.	%	No.	%
1) My action can make a real difference to the environment.	368	30.7	556	46.3	141	11.8	122	10.2	13	1.1	1,200	100.0
2) It is important that people organize themselves into groups to support environmental protection.	392	32.7	632	52.7	127	10.6	42	3.5	7	0.6	1,200	100.0
3) It is important that each of us cares for the environment, even if it takes time.	447	37.3	589	49.1	101	8.4	55	4.6	8	0.7	1,200	100.0
4) It is important that each of us cares for the environment, even if it costs money.	255	21.3	529	44.1	184	15.3	187	15.6	45	3.8	1,200	100.0
5) The Government should reduce environmental problems, but it should not cost me any money.	466	38.8	398	33.2	121	10.1	190	15.8	25	2.1	1,200	100.0
6) It is important that each of us takes part in a campaign to clean up the green areas in the mountains.	425	35.4	548	45.7	144	12.0	57	4.8	26	2.2	1,200	100.0

themselves to take part in a campaign to protect the environment, but they believe that money for environmental protection should come from the government.

Environmental Behavior

To explore the real environmental awareness of Tehran residents, respondents were asked about their daily behavior concerning ten simple actions (Table 7). Picnicking with family and friends, for example, is a common way to spend time over the weekend. Most people responded that they always or almost always clean the picnic areas before leaving and going back home. Another simple daily act is water saving at home, and more than 60 percent of respondents declared that they turn off the faucet while brushing their teeth. Another common action is putting the family garbage on the street only a short time before garbage collection to avoid smell, rats or stray cats: this is done regularly by 58.4 percent of respondents.

Environmental problems are also becoming a relatively frequent matter of conversation. Some respondents say that they always talk about such issues, and more than 50 percent affirm that they talk with friends and relatives about such negative aspects of the modern urban life "most of the time" or "sometimes." A good share of respondents also try to use plastic and paper bags several times, and they also purchase some food items (milk, sodas) in returnable bottles. In both cases, such actions result in some savings to the family. Other acts are much less frequent: separation of papers and bottles for recycling, non-use of the car in case of pollution or respect for speed limits. The motivations for these apparently contradictory behaviors are clear; the first case requires space and organization, while the second and third ones are very difficult to adopt in a so vast metropolis where many people have to commute daily on long distances.

When the answers are analyzed by gender, women almost always seem to perform slightly better than men. Regarding the picnic area, 48.5 percent of men and 55.2 percent of women declared that they always clean up, and for the household garbage, 43.8 percent of men and 46.0 percent of women said that they put it outside on time. 45.1 percent of men and 39.5 percent of women also indicated that they do not leave the faucet running when brushing teeth, in order to save clean water. On recycling-related actions, 41.0 percent of men and 35.7 percent of women said that they never reuse plastic and paper bags, and 41.3 percent of men and 28.0 percent of women declared that they never separate empty bottles, papers and other garbage.

The respondents were also asked if they had done anything in the last three years specifically oriented toward the conservation of nature, the landscape, or the environment. Among the 1,189 people who responded to this question, almost 80 percent recognize that they did not do anything of special value with a slight difference between men and women: 76 percent of men and 81 percent of women confirm their total lack of action with no significant difference among various age groups. By increasing the level of education, however, people indicate more action. Some of the activities indicated by the respondents were a) planting of trees on roadsides and courtyards (11.1 percent) and b) taking part in a campaign to clean a polluted place (3.9 percent), and cleaning streets and alleys (1.8 percent). The membership in environmental groups was declared by only five respondents, 0.4 percent of the total.

Table 7. Environmental Behavior

Statements	Total													
	Always		Most of the Time		Sometimes		Not Applicable		Never		Total	
	No.	%	No.	%	No.	%	No.	%	No.	%	No.	%
1) I put house garbage outside the door on time.	540	45.0	161	13.4	301	25.1	143	11.9	55	4.6	1,200	100.0
2) I reuse plastic and paper bags.	199	16.6	286	23.8	185	15.4	68	5.7	462	38.5	1,200	100.0
3) When air is polluted, I do not use my car.	129	10.8	206	17.2	115	9.6	595	49.6	155	12.9	1,200	100.0
4) When I brush my teeth, I do not leave the faucet running.	508	42.3	213	17.8	249	20.8	44	3.7	186	15.5	1,200	100.0
5) I drive to keep my fuel consumption as low as possible.	240	20.0	152	12.7	144	12.0	590	49.2	74	6.2	1,200	100.0
6) I buy milk and Coke in returnable containers.	325	27.1	302	25.2	246	20.5	125	10.4	202	16.8	1,200	100.0
7) I respect speed limits on freeways.	290	24.2	107	8.9	167	13.9	561	46.8	75	6.3	1,200	100.0
8) I separate empty bottles, papers and other garbage.	217	18.1	298	24.8	171	14.3	98	8.2	416	34.7	1,200	100.0
9) After a picnic, I leave the place as it was originally.	621	51.8	200	16.7	241	20.1	58	4.8	80	6.7	1,200	100.0
10) I talk with my friends about environmental problems.	192	16.0	463	38.6	144	12.0	75	6.3	326	27.2	1,200	100.0

15

Knowledge of the Authority Responsible for Monitoring Air Pollution

About 58 percent of respondents do not know which authority is responsible for monitoring air pollution, while 8 percent declared that there is no authority responsible (Table 8).

Among the 34 percent of men and women who declared knowledge, 67 percent mentioned the DOE. More precisely, 60 percent mentioned the DOE on its own, 3 percent mentioned it together with the MOT and 4 percent together with an air quality control company.

Of the respondents, the age group between 51 and 60 is more likely to know the authority responsible (48 percent), followed by those over 60 (37 percent), and then by those between 21 and 30 (37 percent). Taking gender into consideration, 27 percent of women answered, "Yes, I know," versus 42 percent of male respondents. The place of residence has a moderate impact in the awareness of the respondents. The influence of education on responses follows the expected direction: 67 percent of those polled with a post-graduate education declared to know who is responsible, decreasing to 48 percent for bachelor's degree holders, and 30 percent for diploma holders. The two groups of people who are only literate (13 percent) and illiterate (9 percent) represent the lowest percentages.

The role of occupation is also important in determining knowledge of the authority responsible for monitoring air pollution: 75 percent of top managers and 59 percent of the specialists affirm knowledge with the lowest percentage shown by jobless respondents (21 percent). The relationship with income follows in the expected direction: people surveyed with the highest income are more informed than those with lowest revenues. Membership in an environmental organization demonstrates a much more informed respondent, but unfortunately only 21 people out of the 1,200 interviewed fall in this category.

For knowledge of the agency responsible for air quality monitoring, Univariate Logit model estimates of the probability of positive response can be summarized as follows: the socioeconomic variables that have a significant influence in the studied phenomenon are gender, age, education and occupation. Concerning gender, there is a significant difference in answering "Yes" between men and women: the estimated probability for women is 0.27 (p-value $= 0.00$) and for men is 0.42 (p-value $= 0.00$). The estimated probability of answering "Yes" is a quadratic function of age, the interpretation of which indicates young people have a quite low estimated probability of knowledge (for a person aged 20 is equal to 0.28). The estimated probability increases with age (for age 50 it is 0.45) and mildly decreases around age 60 (for age 65 it is 0.44).

With regard to education, people with levels of education in the categories of illiterate, literate, primary school, secondary school, high school and religious education seem

Table 8. Knowledge of Authority Responsible for Monitoring Air Pollution, by Gender

	Total					
	Men		Women		Total	
Responses	No.	%	No.	%	No.	%
Yes, I know	255	42.1	157	27.1	412	34.8
No, I don't know	303	50.0	379	65.5	682	57.6
No one	48	7.9	43	7.4	91	7.6
Total	606	100.0	579	100.0	1185	100.0

Table 9. Knowledge about Authority Responsible for Monitoring Water Pollution

	Total					
	Male		Female		Total	
Statement	No.	%	No.	%	No.	%
Yes, I know	304	50.3	247	42.7	551	46.6
No, I do not know	263	43.5	302	52.2	565	47.8
No one	37	6.1	30	5.2	67	5.7
Total	604	100.0	579	100.0	1,183	100.0

to have homogeneous behavior and their estimated probability of answering "Yes" is low (0.29, p-value = 0.00). The estimated probability increases significantly for people with a bachelor's degree (0.48, p-values = 0.00) and for post-graduate education and PhD holders (0.65, p-value = 0.00). With respect to occupation, people who work in their own homes, jobless, industrial workers and students, exhibit homogenous behavior (estimated probability 0.28, p-value = 0.00). A significant increase in the estimated probability is shown for public employees (0.40, p-value = 0.00) and private employees (0.39, p-value = 0.00). The estimated probability for specialists is 0.57 (p-value = 0.00); while for top managers it is 0.75 (p-value 0.00).

The estimated probability of answering "Yes" to knowledge of the air quality monitoring agency varies significantly with income: people with no income show the lowest level (0.26, p-value = 0.00). For people with income below 1 thousand rials, the estimated probability goes up to 0.37 (p-value = 0.00), and to 0.36 (p-value = 0.00) for people with income between 1 million and 2 million rials. For people with income between 2 million and 3 million rials, it is equal to 0.51 (p-value = 0.00). For people with income between 3 million and 4 million it is 0.46 (p-value = 0.00) while for people with income above 4 million it is 0.55 (p-value = 0.00).

The logit model with the explanatory variable, membership of an environmental organization was not considered due to the small number of people in this group.

Knowledge about responsibility for monitoring water pollution (Table 9) is better than that of air pollution with 50.3 percent of men and 42.7 percent of women declaring knowledge of which authority is responsible for this activity. About 78.6 percent and 83.9 percent of them respectively answered that it is the duty of Water Company and Waste Water Company. There seems to be little difference among the responses of various age groups, however, again there is a link between education level and this answer.

Behavior in Case of an Environmental Problem: To File or Not to File a Complaint?

In case of an environmental problem, only 32 percent of respondents affirm that they would react and inform the authorities. The Municipality of Tehran (MOT) is widely recognized as being in charge of environmental problems: out of the above-mentioned active minority, 59 percent would address themselves to the MOT and only 21 percent to the DOE. In addition, another 6 percent mention the MOT, together with other agencies.

Table 10. File of Formal Complaint in Case of Environmental Contamination, by Gender

Responses	Male		Female		Total	
	No.	%	No.	%	No.	%
Yes	185	30.3	200	34.5	385	32.4
No	425	69.7	380	65.5	805	67.6
Total	610	100.0	580	100.0	1,190	100.0

Of women, 34.5 percent are likely to file a complaint if they witness environmental contamination versus 30.3 percent of the male respondents (Table 10). Respondents under age 20 are relatively likely (37 percent), followed by those between ages 51 and 60 (37 percent), while the elderly show the lowest percentage. Of the people living in the southern part of Tehran, 36 percent would file a complaint, whereas only about 30 percent of the residents in both the central and northern part of town would do so.

The role of education in the likelihood to file a complaint is not linear: holders of graduate degrees and those with secondary education indicate active behavior with 44 percent declaring intention to file. The probability of least active behavior is declared by people with a bachelor degree (29 percent). People with different occupations declare different attitudes about the environmental problems, which may reflect their daily experiences and their consequent rationalization of the environmental problems they encounter. Top managers are very likely to file a complaint (63 percent), followed by industrial workers (48 percent), whereas the categories with the lowest active behavior are the jobless (25 percent), private employees (25 percent) and students (27 percent). The relationship between income and behavior is not very linear, because people with relatively lower incomes declare behavior similar to that of richer groups. In case of environmental problems, membership in an environmental organization determines a much more active behavior: 52 percent of this category would file a complaint in the case of an environmental problem versus 32 percent of the non-members. Unfortunately, only 21 people fall in this category of the 1,200 interviewed.

Area of residence and occupation are the only significant socioeconomic variables indicated by the Univariate Logit model estimates of the probability of filing a complaint in case of an observed environmental problem. In relation to residence, people who live in North and Center of Teheran have an estimated probability of a positive answer of 0.30 (p-value = 0.00). There is a significant increase of this probability in people living in South Tehran (0.36, p-value = 0.094) and non-residents in Teheran (0.46, p-value = 0.054).

Concerning occupation, the logit analysis suggests that respondents who are housewives, top managers and industrial workers have the highest estimated probability of a positive answer for filing a complaint of 0.38 (p-value = 0.00). There is a significant decrease of the estimated probability of a positive answer for those who are jobless (0.25, p-value = 0.015), for students (0.27, p-value = 0.010), and for private employees (0.27, p-value 0.012). Membership in environmental organizations was not considered by the analysis, due to the extremely small number of respondents in this category.

Table 11. Most Appreciated Information Source, by Gender

Source	Average°	Men	Women	Z-value[1]	P-value[2]
Schools	5.845	5.970	5.713	1.361	0.173
MOT	6.026	5.941	6.101	−0.824	0.410
DOE	6.815	6.646	6.991	−1.925	0.054
NGOs	3.367	3.313	3.423	−0.642	0.521
Mosques	3.242	3.105	3.385	−1.390	0.164

Notes:
°Values ranging from 0 = minimum to 10 = maximum;
[1]Z-value: Under the null hypothesis that the population means of men and women are equal (Unequal variances assumed);
[2]P-value: Probability of observing a larger Z-value (in module) under the null hypothesis.

Information Sources and Channels

There are various information sources on environmental issues available in Teheran. The most important of them were assumed to be schools and universities, the Municipality of Teheran (MOT), the Department of Environment (DOE), NGOs, mosques, etc. Respondents were asked to rate between 0 and 10 (0 for lack of trust, 10 for complete trust) to express their level of trust on these information sources. Achieving an average score of 6.81/10 (Table 11), the DOE appears to be the most highly trusted source of environmental information by people surveyed.

The MOT and the school system rank in the second and third positions with 6.03/10 and 5.84/10 respectively. It is disappointing, but to some extent expected, that 25.9 percent of respondents rated NGOs as zero as sources of information on environmental issues. Gender differences do not appear to be significant, with the DOE as the only exception, for which the negative difference between the score given by men and women can be considered meaningful (p-value = 0.054).

The DOE has a better image with older people and with respondents of lower education, being highly appreciated by 48 percent of those between the ages of 61 and 70; whereas only 31 percent of the respondents under 20 and only 27 percent of the age group 21–30 express the same judgment. Only 27 percent of people with bachelor's degrees and 19 percent with postgraduate or PhD degrees completely trust the DOE. This figure is much higher for the other classes of respondents with a minor level or no education.

Regarding the relationship between Tehran residents and the several existing information channels, the survey finds television to be the most trusted information channel for environmental information (Table 12), receiving a mean score of 7.33/10. More than 33 percent of respondents completely rely on television.

Radio ranks in second position (6.39) and newspapers (5.94) in third. Women appear to rely on all of these information channels more than men, with the exception of newspapers; however, differences appear to be significant only regarding billboards (p-value = 0.000), conferences and fairs (p-value = 0.005), Internet (p-value = 0.032), family and friends (p-value = 0.035), and books (p-value = 0.045).

Table 12. Most Appreciated Information Channel, by Gender

Channel	Average°	Men	Women	Z-value[1]	P-value[2]
Newspapers	5.940	6.040	5.854	1.012	0.310
Magazines	5.303	5.149	5.464	1.828	0.067
Television	7.331	7.220	7.447	−1.384	0.166
Radio	6.388	6.303	6.478	−0.951	0.342
Family and friends	4.487	4.300	4.684	−2.107	0.035
Books	5.715	5.538	5.900	−2.006	0.045
Internet	5.512	5.297	5.739	−2.139	0.032
Conferences and fairs	5.159	4.902	5.428	−2.784	0.005
Clergy	2.395	2.249	2.548	−1.691	0.091
Billboards	4.872	4.569	5.191	−3.561	0.000
Cinemas	3.285	3.228	3.345	−0.630	0.529

Notes:
°Values ranging from 0 = minimum to 10 = maximum;
[1]Z-value: Under the null hypothesis that the population means of men and women are equal (Unequal variances assumed);
[2]P-value: Probability of observing a larger Z-value (in module) under the null hypothesis.

Young and middle-aged people watch TV more than older respondents. Illiterate people rely highly on the clergy—much more than on written information channels, such as newspapers, books, magazines, Internet, and so forth. Respondents with lower education prefer to receive this kind of information through clergy, TV, or radio.

Among the many TV channels available to Tehran residents, 39 percent of respondents highly prefer Channel 3 and 27 percent prefer Tehran Channel. Furthermore, there is a gender difference: 36 percent of women chose Tehran Channel but only 19 percent of men, while 45 percent of men chose Channel 3 and only 33 percent of women. Illiterate, literate and people with primary school education prefer to watch Channel 3 and Channel 1. Respondents with secondary and high school, diploma, bachelor, postgraduate and PhD degrees prefer Channel 3 and Tehran Channel.

Among different radio stations, Sport station, Tehran station, and Health station rank in the top three positions respectively with 40, 14, and 12 percent of respondents affirming themselves as listeners. Payam station finds itself at the lowest position with 3.4 percent. About 42.3 percent of women prefer Sport station and 15.2 percent Tehran station, while 38.4 percent of men prefer Sport station, 12 percent Tehran station, and 11.5 percent Health station. There is no significant difference among the various age groups or education levels with respect to the available radio stations. The first option for everyone is the Sport station.

Tehran residents read various daily newspapers. The ones most read by the respondents are *Hamshahri* and *Jaam-e-Jam*, with 29 percent and 18 percent respectively. Iran newspaper with 8.7 percent of readers ranks in third position. *Hamshahri* is usually read by 30.1 percent of women and 27.4 percent of men, and *Jam-e-Jam* by 18.2 and 18.5 percent respectively. There is no significant difference between respondents by age and education, as far as readership of dailies is concerned. The only exception is that people with religious education usually prefer to read *Keyhan* and *Aftabe Yazd*.

Among weekly magazines, *Khanevade Sabz* (13.8 percent) is the most important: about 19 percent of women and 9 percent of men usually read this weekly magazine. On the other hand, it was found that 65 percent of respondents do not read any weekly magazine. This characterizes most of the elderly people and particularly those with religious education.

More than 90 percent of respondents—particularly the elderly, those with religious education and with low level of education—do not read any monthly magazine. *Movafaghiat* is the only monthly journal with good circulation: 3.4 percent of women and 1.8 percent of men declare themselves regular readers. Very few people read other monthly magazines.

The survey also investigated several other information channels. Respondents indicate, to varying degrees, that family members, as well as friends or neighbors, are an important vehicles of environmental information. The Internet is highly ranked by the younger strata. Conferences, fairs, exhibitions, and festivals are also relevant information channels and are ranked very positively by many respondents. As far as environmental information is concerned, the clergy is not considered an important channel. Billboards located along the main roads of the town are relatively relevant, while cinemas are not considered very important.

CHAPTER 4

Conclusions

The results of this study show that for Tehran residents the environment is not yet thought to be an important problem, when compared with other social and economic issues. When specifically asked about their daily experience with the environment, however, it becomes clear that most people do worry about the quality of air and water. This consciousness does not translate into real actions, because only a tiny minority participates in the activities of environmental groups and very few respondents affirm to have done something positive in relation to environment. This lack of action is partially due to the belief that environmental protection should be the government's duty, more than an individual's responsibility. The absence of advocacy organizations and the scarce activism of the existing environmental organizations are other relevant factors, which explain the tiny fraction of respondents belonging to such advocacy movements.

Socioeconomic factors, such as education, income and occupation, affect responses generally in expected directions. Few respondents, however, are able to indicate clearly which authority is responsible for air quality control and for the diffusion of data regarding air quality. Strangely enough, people with low levels of education appreciate the DOE more than those with better education and higher incomes. The relatively poor attention of students towards environmental problems is another factor that emerged from the study and could call for careful consideration.

In addition, the study confirms the need for a properly focused information campaign to raise the level of knowledge about the environment and to form the consciousness that could motivate people to act or to accept the changes imposed by the authorities. The study also found that several information channels need to be used in order to reach different groups of Tehran residents. Fortunately, there is a wealth of media and the most appropriate ones can be selected to target specific content and groups.

References

Arcury, T.A., and T.A. Johnson T.A. 1987. "Public environmental knowledge: a state-wide survey." *Journal of Environmental Education* 18:31–37.

Buttel, F.H., and P. Taylor. 1979. "Environmental sociology and global environmental change: a critical assessment." In M. Redclift and T. Benton, eds. *Social theory and the global environment.* London: Routledge.

Cottrell, S.P., and A.R. Graefe. 1997. "Testing a conceptual framework of responsible environmental behavior." *Journal of Environmental Education* 29(1):17–27.

Dunlap, R.E., and others. 1978. "The new environmental paradigm." *Journal of Environmental Education* 9(Summer):10–19.

Keiser, F.G., S. Woelfing, and U. Fuhrer. 1999. "Environmental attitude and ecological behaviour." *Journal of Environmental Psychology* 19:1–19.

Hansen, M.H., W.N. Hurwitz, and W.G. Madow. 1953. *Sample survey methods and theory.* Vol. I: Methods and Applications. New York: Wiley.

Laws, S., C. Harper, and R. Marcus. 2003. *Research for development.* London: SAGE Publications Ltd.

McFarland, B., and P. Boxall. 2003. "The role of social psychological and social structural variables in environmental activism: an example of the forest sector." *Journal of Environmental Psychology* 23:79–87.

Schultz, P.W., and L.C. Zelezny. 1999. "Value as predictors of environmental attitudes: evidence for consistency across cultures." *Journal of Environmental Psychology* 19:255–65.

Stern, P., and others. 1993. "Value orientations, gender, and environmental concern." *Environment and behavior* 25(3):322–48.

Tuna, M. 2004. "Public environmental attitudes in Turkey." In C. Phillips, ed., *Environmental Justice and Global Citizenship.* Oxford: The Interdisciplinary Press.

Eco-Audit

Environmental Benefits Statement

The World Bank is committed to preserving Endangered Forests and natural resources. We print World Bank Working Papers and Country Studies on 100 percent postconsumer recycled paper, processed chlorine free. The World Bank has formally agreed to follow the recommended standards for paper usage set by Green Press Initiative—a nonprofit program supporting publishers in using fiber that is not sourced from Endangered Forests. For more information, visit www.greenpressinitiative.org.

In 2007, the printing of these books on recycled paper saved the following:

Trees*	Solid Waste	Water	Net Greenhouse Gases	Total Energy
264	12,419	96,126	23,289	184 mil.
'40' in height and 6–8" in diameter	Pounds	Gallons	Pounds CO_2 Equivalent	BTUs

green press
INITIATIVE